PIONEER VALLEY EDUCAT

DOLPHINS

MICHÈLE DUFRESNE

Here is a dolphin.

Dolphins live in the sea, but they are not fish. Dolphins are mammals, like humans.

Dolphins like to eat fish and squid.
This dolphin is looking for some fish to eat.

Dolphins like to play.
They like to jump
out of the water.

Look at this dolphin jumping out of the water.

Dolphins have a blowhole to get air.

Here is a mother
and a baby dolphin.
A mother dolphin will stay
with a baby dolphin
for two to three years.

mammals

blowhole

dolphin

squid